Photo Credit: Gunther Wilhelm

berni m janssen, a text artist, works with words in all their forms: printed, spoken, performed. She has a collaborative multidisciplinary practice spanning over thirty-five years, working with composers, performers, visual artists and community members to make word inspired art. She is renowned for her evocative and captivating performances.

The passion began with poems, and poems in books: *Possessives and Plurals* (Fillia Press, 1985); *Xstatic* (Post Neo, 1988); *mangon* (Mercurial Editions, 1992) and *Lake & Vale* (PressPress, 2010). Poems have been published in magazines including *Cordite, Heat, Meanjin, Overland Extra* and performed on radio and around the world.

also by berni m janssen

Lake & Vale (PressPress, 2010)

mangon (Mercurial Editions, 1992)

xstatic (Post Neo, 1988)

Possessives and Plurals (Fillia Press, 1985)

works in anthologies

La Traducterie (Australian Poets Today, 2008)

Neustra Voz (Biblioteca de Textos Universitarios of the Universidad Católica de Salta, 2005)

She's Fantastical: The First Anthology of Australian Women's Speculative Fiction, Magical Realism and Fantasy (Eds. Lucy Sussex and Judith Raphael Buckrich, Sybylla Feminist Press, 1995)

Poetry and Gender: Statements and Essays in Australian Women's Poetry and Poetics (Eds. David Brooks and Brenda Walker, UQP, 1989)

Soft Lounges (Eds. Antonia Bruns and John Jenkins, Fringe Network, 1984)

between wind and water

(in a vulnerable place)

berni m janssen

SPINIFEX

First published by Spinifex Press, 2018

Spinifex Press Pty Ltd
PO Box 5270, North Geelong, Victoria 3215
PO Box 105, Mission Beach, Queensland 4852
Australia

women@spinifexpress.com.au
www.spinifexpress.com.au

Acknowledgements

'words on wind ears wide open', 'Fay speaks volumes' and 'Leon' have been published in OZBURP-5.

Cover design: Deb Snibson
Typesetting: Helen Christie
Typeset in Adobe Garamond Pro
Printed by McPherson's Printing Group

 A catalogue record for this book is available from the National Library of Australia

Paperback   9781925581591
ePub   9781925581621
Adobe PDF   9781925581607
Kindle   9781925581614

This project has been assisted by the Australian Government through the Australia Council, its principal arts funding and advisory body.

For

Gunther

And all those who do not accept injustice
who reveal, name, resist and fight it.

thank you

To the many people over the years that I have met, heard, heard of, or heard from, many brave people who have told their stories in the hope that something will be done, so that other people will not have to suffer what they have suffered. They not only live close to industrial wind complexes but close to mines, power plants and other sources of industrial noise. Also the compassionate, courageous people who have stood with, supported and assisted them. It is their stories and courage that have inspired this work.

There are so many ways people have contributed to the making of this work, from the seemingly offhand remark, answers for niggly questions, conversations, inquiry, feedback and support. Thank you to each and every one of you.

Thank you to Donald Thomas for sharing his knowledge of local customary.

Thank you to Gunther Wilhelm for his support, love and patience through the many years.

Thank you to Catherine Schieve for her Afterword, a thoughtful weave of impressions spanning many years and spaces.

Thank you to Susan Hawthorne and Renate Klein for their support of the work and their insightful editorial advice.

I acknowledge the Dja Dja Wurrung People of the Kulin Nation, traditional owners of country where I live and work, and pay my respect to them, their culture and their Elders past, present and future.

contents

Words, cast them to the wind.

(Portuguese proverb)

STILL

still

this soil flesh mine fragile beneath rock-bone harder than hard forged over
a long age a great heat slow cool mica quartz feldspar grains coarse and
compose rain wind shape exposed softer wash and wear disperse soles pad
pause deliberate take two two feet plant not harsh thought action cleft in this
ooze of time snooze slow and slow a low growing with spring fall broken a
patch a pitch and sometimes some sweet succulence scents sent on whispers
wind curling

kangaroo grass spear grass

      soft spear grass spurred spear grass

          plump spear grass quizzical spear-grass

            wallaby grass velvet wallaby grass

              bristly wallaby grass grey tussock grass

                  windmill grass weeping love grass

    noah's ark

not about time not clock ticketh human defined not time never enough
of human short-lived obsess complain about time my being is before hand
clock beyond tick tock a long slow present wearing tempo of sun moon stars
planets mantle rub rock shift plates shelves rock a by by n by bye bye a great
cycling some belly core breath easing the seasons into place the sun earth
breathing a shimmering breath starspan breath longer than a human's breath
with this breathing I have found a repose in which my skin wears gradual as
rock it is this vantage point that I wish to share with you as one who sits in a
skin of rock of dust of an age untold of one who has seen those aerial bodies
for millions of cycles and will as they turn and their glimmer expires

wirilda   prickly moses

hairy sheep's burr   bidgee-widgee

rock quillwort   black anther flax lily

feather heads   dusty miller

honey-pots   mountain beauty

golden weather glass   austral grass tree

blunt everlasting

small feet tickle my dust print into decay a lace of living strung from tails swooping bounding swishing surface to air fleet the colour the pattern the texture each to their own and of their passing they home in me guests homebodies storm swept vagrants all murmur stories in tracks and tales find sustenance sanctuary

black wallaby   grey kangaroo

echidna   antechinus   *tiger snake   eastern brown*

little eagle   willie wagtail   *magpie   kookaburra*

powerful owl bearded dragon   *shingleback skink*

firm tread presses this skin cracked and rock-tempered the stepping is in tune they know the other well the other of their country of their kind they are living in the stepping together all in step singing some low slow walk talk easing the tread into earth they carry the bundles of their lives this walking watching walking treading stepping walking over the moon cycling over and over the moon cycling long tracks worn with steps like rain like wind this wear a soft worn down rounded as vowels sung hung in the air stretched by wind I too am well rounded this rounding a love a love around splendour thing more than hills mammary memories this love sung strong strung mama mewling child the milk breast warm

red box	*grey box*
yellow box	*long leaved box*
messmate	*manna*
drooping she-oak	*red stringybark*
yellow gum	*silver banksia*
red gum	*golden wattle*

acacia paradoxa

4

before shoes soles we skin to skin both rock hardened both cracked when the bare flesh knows ground home I have heard the dreams such soft night murmurings the moon brush stroke light dabbled all played out in the space of breath and earth dreams though the dreams though eat stars and traverse plains country I have never seen I am a homebody anchored not storm troubled but troubles are trebling

hairy buttons

blowfly grass

tall blue bells

scarlet sundew

golden everlasting

greenhoods golden

billy buttons

guildford grass

sweet bursaria

brome fescue

common rice

flower early

nancies pale

rush rigid

panic spiny

grasses

xanthorrhoea

many a plant has found sustenance in the slender cracks of my aging nestling in scurf homed in wrinkle though the flesh not supple then pickets and posts driven in (they sweated over that winter or summer as they should) to mark boundaries declare ownership a path between the flock of huts out yonder and the line of shops back there was trudged and ridden for a bag of flour sugar tea company the fall on stony outcrop over dust twig tussock snake booze butterfly clouds bruised remembrance not all flesh is forgiving

masked wood swallow   *red wattle bird*

striated pardalote   *green grass parrot*   *little corella*   *magpie lark*

white winged chough   *common bronzewing*

nankeen kestrel   *brown goshawk*   *raven*   *superb fairy wren*

white throated tree creeper

I have observed all manner of things in this passing of the cycles humans
who have stridden run ridden driven humans who have laughed shouted
cried screamed gurgled murmured humans who have raged desired
humans dug holes scraped and scratched driven stakes with gnarled and
deformed emotions their hands rigid with despair humans who have
lost hope heart husband wife child lost and empty seeking some seeking
much some much more much much more ah let us talk of greed that
which I have seen many manifestations many manifestations here I too
know despair but what of despair in an old rock tears cannot crumble
from my interior long squeezed out in a hardness not of spirit but of
form a hard rock endures all except greed which can rip the heart out
of any living and it is greed that I see tear and desecrate destroy and
plunder

black swans

eurasian coots   *spoonbills*

straw-necked ibises   *grey egrets*

little pied cormorant   *white faced herons*

musk ducks   *shelducks*   *teal ducks*   *wood ducks*   *black fronted dotterel*   *masked lapwing*

pick and axe pick away at my skin score my flesh destroy seeds wheedle into
oh the small gaps but pick tine mattock spade gash scar nowhere deep as
ploughshears dynamite dozers drill rigs excavators now this bobcat not catlike
has tyred teeth crunch in does not bob lightly on my skin pinch scrape rip
shred all torn from this old stone where crevices of dirt harboured small life
rootclung water sung cycle upon cycle they stretch into the sun and wind
earth held growing with measured draughts small seeds unfurled to a tall
presence hundreds of moon cycles to grow their grandeur before the sun sets
they lie sundried who will remember them?

tallsundew plainquillwort toughscurfpea wirybuttons drumsticks
rabbitears hairybeardheath milkmaids tigerorchid chocolatelily pinkfingers yamdaisies

there be gold diggers all time take and take extracting without heart thought respect leave their broken backs broken dreams all broken this skin scratched and scarred pocked with desperation all those stepping in tune singing moved on moved out crushed in the pounding desire pounding flesh skin for more more much more a chant on the wind on the breath pummelling

galah sulfur crested cockatoo red browed finch welcome swallow eastern
spinebill yellow tufted honeyeaters grey shrike thrush scarlet robin crimson
rosella musk lorikeet red rumped parrot painted button quail wedge tail
eagle brolga barking owl

there are farmers and there are farmers it has always been that way some tune to the ground the seasons the air all the animals living around movements songs and sounds signalling rain the best time to plant some sense the rhythms know it as their blood others do not for whatever reason others see the more more more score of cleft hooved scouring ground dust dry ringing up quick fortune they dream in numbers others do as others do

whoo   whooooooo   whooooo
whoo hoo hoo
wheit wheit tseit tseit

folk with dreams familiar folk urgent for dreams embodiment abundant folk with patient perseverance to birth dreams few folk with luck needed for dreams realisation fewer disappointment is often carried

aier-ek aier-rr k aer rk errk urrk aiirk
airrrik aarrrk ahrk aieirrk aieirieik

water slicking granite gathering into mud the careful hope of farmers gardeners
and the parched roos seek water in cracks crevices succulents those planted in
gardens tended tendered attended a little grey water sparing anxiety is born in
the seasons any one and nurtured there by any one but this long stint rain dry
dust foment cracked the skin the membrane containing laughter and deep
nostalgia children splashing water drops sun spangled water arcing at dusk
into mosquito hummed bed vegetal fragrance full a long shower on a hot day
these seasons have come and gone

chirrink chirrink   chirrink chirrink
chiak chiak chak chak
ktee tip k tee tip k tee it tip kteeit tip tip tee

days and nights when the peace returns are precious returning
to an earlier time not so long ago in the scheme of my existing
a peace where quivering air trembling soil a thudding and
humming do not occupy the land this land of our breathing
quiet of our somnolent state a state of meditation of eyes
wide open aware of trees plants animals breathing of birds
and bees yes of birds and bees to hear their quiet song
their particular song their chirrup of conversation melancholy
monologues to their dying note ah for days such as these where
voices are unstrung today is such a day blessed equally by
exquisite intersection of sunlight soft as in autumn evenings
and blue skies blue as the calls of choughs like children lost a blue
to fall somersaulting as feathers light and quixotic we die in this peace

tzeck tchek
aairk aarh aarh aargagh
chit twit tswit chat tsweeit
whitchety wheit
whitch i wheit whitchit

8

cherish this earth blessed day be brown bristle blazed and bleached dry
the crisp edge of blue anchors my uprising how the voice jellied finds
form quakes my rock inclines gulch gulf between one wave and the next
pound the day to dust the body to dust the smallest particle windblown
flexes flees he steps away he is leaving with his head clutched eyesight
blurred and his feet are not firm on terra as his heart beats rapid more
rapid as the world swirls smudged glyphs of a landscape he knows too
well dots on t's clots on clods of hooves tapping out code more code he
heard this disjunction this gulf of blur and swirl and a tattoo of heart
where all was still and steady he is not firm in his ways now he strays
thoughts stray and he pins them small scraps (notes) inside his boots
move the sheep from the top paddock notes of the day in his top pocket
a tiny book inscribed tiny script the volume is up noting the weather
wind and turbines noting

The wind sweeping through the tower
heralds a rising storm in the mountains.

(Chinese proverb)

TURN

in this rural idyll

sheep fleck rollicking hills in baa loads
                              red earth havens spuds
        black cattle barge brown cattle shuffle all heads down
                                   a stiff wind slants surfaces

              farmers gaze to the future heroic hand
                 shading eyes standing over the dry dry land
                    cry cry crying water cash flow wanting
        diesel fertiliser sheep grain spuds price capricious as wind
        rain weather blow hot cold out of their hands

clouds of dust sheep hooves ground down ground dust
        paddocks of paddocks of
                wind-whipped flurry of
                dust worry

        in this rural idyll a bright golden age promised
        one hundred and fifty years of farming nous harvested
        from the old country where water and soil are deep
        15 drought years stripped this already weatherworn
        crust bone bare
        the whip of wind sun
        earth salt man lives cracks

the skin of farmers furrowed burnt their eyes ablaze
with hunger suck in the revolutionary spin
they are saved cash will flow if the creeks will not

The Company seeks

There is a great art in selling the wind. (Spanish proverb)

Team* seeks open and honest* dialogue*
with landowners neighbours and other land users
building* meaningful* relationships* through community* relations* plan*
targeted* engagement* community* consultation* long before any
approval understand* and respond* to all
concerns* work* with individuals and communities*
reach mutually acceptable* positive* outcomes* promote* our core
business* benefits* develop* better level* of understanding* co-operation*
and engagement* with our communities.*

*weasel words

Basic unit of corporatism of The Company 'seeks' open and honest in the context of the situation at a particular point of time that is not necessarily this one, honest in all but a few non essential details talks discussions chats with individuals they are aiming to bring on board, within the local district (before the project becomes public and before anyone knows anything and can ask too many questions or object) who will benefit from the commercial operations who will then be known as 'the community' and who The Company will enter into secret binding agreements (before the project has become public and before anyone knows anything and can ask too many questions or object).

The other people in the district who on certain occasions or situations that The Company publicist or community liaison manager deems beneficial to The Company will be known as 'the community'. It is this 'community' that the basic unit of corporatism of The Company want to charm persuade enlist involve get onside keep onside bring over win bamboozle inveigle into dupe get on board read from the same page sing the same tune through meetings and information sessions where the basic unit of corporatism of The Company tells 'the community' the relevant information, that is the information that The Company wants 'the community' to know regarding the project. As these meetings are consultation sessions, so that the basic unit of corporatism of The Company will better know what is on the minds of the people who are other than those who are financially benefitting from the projects, minimal time is made available at the end of the sessions for questions and comments, if there are any after the informative information has been provided. Members of 'the community' may require further information, ask probing questions be critical of the project or object. The basic unit of corporatism of The Company will cozen con fool trick win flatter deceive bamboozle fob inveigle into dupe hoodwink gull bluff play for a sucker intimidate to ensure questions and objections will be answered in due course in a manner deemed appropriate in protecting The Company's commercial interests.

Dan and Gaby

he has been a man of fewer words but of late has found
the need to speak those few words always chosen with care
as if he knew the number of words his lifetime could afford
were limited now that he needs must speak this considered
habit of words forms succinct sentences each with the strength
born of attention necessity dictates whilst his speaking
has become voluminous (try to stop his flow!) words are still
deliberated to make the point explain to tell the tale

when in short pants he itched to know the what and how
and why of everything the centipede and whether there
are a hundred legs and do they each step one after
the other or alternate side to side or why it was that oil
floats on water after rain and sun such tiny green filaments
erupt or how the clanking windmill draws the water up into
the dam his curiosity observed and reasoned questions were
as seeds to spring his mind to paddocks of fresh thinking

his curiosity knew no fences as he gathered and pondered he was
not inclined to talk while for many talk is just talk words spilling
without pause or reason Dan distils words some thought a farmers
cautious mind chewing the cud of the day all rumination to sheep and hay not
hearing in his clear articulation the weight of a man planted in the land
the place on which he stands others found in his space the happy chance
for long consideration of weather crop and country of neighbours plight or
fortune advice on pumps and products on wool and wheat of the what

where when who of the everything there is to know to live in these rustic
parts in his top pocket a small notebook holds the details of agricultural
suppliers hay prices rotational grazing rainfall temperatures and tasks all
the minutiae collected reflected upon this year-in-year-out observation of
seasons stock and soil months without rain then torrents then dry and dry
and dry the wind stealing soil seeds withered sheep drenched water carted
stock moved fed in these rhythms note the shift and change attend to the
health of the land knowing the land has been stripped and strained and cannot

cannot continue this way now plant fast growing acacias spiny hakea wind
breaks grow the grass to suit the soil not alter the soil to suit the grass
cocksfoot phleris fescue spineless burr medock perennial rye grass many
deep rooted tapping subsoil damp many fix nitrogen thrive in acidic
soil minimal till drill the seed fold in harvest stubble rotate crops manure
sheep camp on the highest ground bring nutrients up flow down when
the rain when the rain breaks the season not the heart with summer wet dry
winter whenever whatever Dan wanting life to come steward of the land

Dan stands with his wife and children the wind knives their backs
gazes across hill roll to majestic white towers wind spun blades
turning turning turning now into this is the way of the future Dan
says over two hundred country clicks on a Sunday afternoon to set
eyes upon this new horizon their neighbour soon to be the great white
towers flashing arms crest a way away gleam with promise the family
hope into dream in the sun flicking late of day a world renewed where
lives lived full prosperous happy time without end forever and a day

Mitzi and George

He who blows into the wind gets smoke in his eyes. (Slovak proverb)

Round the beer she goes, another round she goes,
she goes round, round, beating a batter
murmuring what matters, what matters.
She's all a chatter, glasses clatter.
Her hands clench the batter beater.

Make better batter to batter better.
Hand clenched misery tooling a bitter food,
she spits, waiting for the splat, the splatter of batter.
She sips, the cook's privilege, she sips, the cook's need.
Cooking such a sweat-laden task, she gulps.
A lick, a sip, clamped lips. She counts.

Days, dollars, desires. Moments. Beaten.
She has frayed edges with worrying. Scurrying
thoughts, rounding the balance, fermenting.
The batter is better for the waiting. Slow rise,
slow fall, as if breathing, as if reliving. Each day
dollars accumulate, desire bubbles.

A small life in a bowl, knows the round, the round
she goes, the glass raised, the glass tossed, the eyes
glazed, the dollars sing, her days ring, desire flattens.
Her hand melds misery, the knife, she mutters.
Make the batter, make the batter, bitter. Scowl,

the furrows ploughed in his brow. Wind hardened.
Eyes flint. His words spare, dint. He counts.
He does not sing, his ears ring. Around, around.
His boot jabs dog. His boot pounds dust.
His thirst a must. This dust, this glare, an horizon stare.
No hill windrow topped, no spot of shimmering gum.

Round, round, they go. She spits. He hits. They blue.
The batter blackens, takes a sickly hue. She
mutters. He stumbles. They grope. She does not
cope. The beater hand clenched. He
falls slowly. She rises. His face pillow slumped,
snoring. She chops. The pillow tears, feathers air.
A small groan. She counts. The split

of seconds. The axe misplaced. The heads hurt,
not harmed. They go round the morning
table, a round of tea, of toast, armed. She takes
the bowl, the glass, the tasks, and asks
what is the matter? what is the matter?

the daily parrot

Every wind is against a leaky ship. (Danish proverb)

at the end of the day when all is said and done
on what side of history particularly you stand and sing
from the daily sheet spin doctors composed
guarantee opinion leaders parrot at this point of time
PM moving forward core promises hip pocket credit
card shopping cart mac mansion aspirational people moving
SUVs double layered pram ordinary Aussie battler
backyards safe in the hands the minds the hearts
of those singing the daily song in pitch in
harmony on message with the pollsters latest tip
over the glass half full/empty government
imminent puts in place no quick fix suite long overdue
wide-ranging reform processes competitive environment roadmap
structural adjustment subsidies tax breaks bottom
line basically growing corporations trickledown jobs
jobs casually churn more jobs keep economy steaming
ahead upside doing it hard large corporations actualise billions
profit while at the drop of the proverbial, sack, oh,
downsize/rightsize as if on a diet workers diet not shareholders
blue chip interest top line growth choice expands better stakeholder
outcomes at the end of the day the politicians future direction
big fat pensions gold cards offshore fly
on holidays to warm swaying palm and pina
colada sands with their extended families
who yawn and swim and complain about
the damn service not being up to scratch. quite frankly.

Dan's notes: early spring

stars frost crystal night
southwest rains once touched ground here
now clouds on horizon

9 ml overnight
first buds bloom dams creek low
no water for fires

north westerly overcast
remember jot notes in small book
heart beats simple

this morning dew glow
ringing and clicking in ears
dizzy fall off truck

still night snaps cold clear
awake quick heart mind racing
turbines gearbox grinds

southwest wind thumping
in shearing shed ears buzz drone
shift sheep to top paddock

Angie and Conrad

one night, when the nights were black without the bleed,

the bleed of city, town or village, lights

that is, not the body scored violent red

without the bleed of light in the vast black, the black tract

of stars infinitesimal, of planets pealing sky, of minds

soaring, of heart's emptying of grief and love and hope,

one night, when the nights were still black, that silent black

as of velvet, as of touch, as of memory,

one night when the stars and moon illuminated a dark sketch of land,

of trees etched on sky, a red light flashed. Flashed again and again.

Flashed in the dark lines of branches, red in the black night.

Danger!   Danger!   Danger!

The swift pound of heart beat cranks up the blood. The ears simmer.

Who goes there?

All is alert.   Panic pummels.   Breath.

Our bed inhabited by the quick dash of fear.

The red mark, the red mark, hits and hits again.

One night, the red lights began to flash.

The red lights atop of towers, flash.   Flash.   Flash.

Danger!   Danger!   Danger!

Red lights punch into our bed, our bodies, our lives.

We are marked and trembling.

This sudden bleed of light, bled from

our lives our haven.

Fay speaks volumes

Tall trees catch much wind. (Dutch proverb)

One of the most common turbines currently in the world

a 1.5 megawatt design.

She said so big I never thought they would be so big.

Each turbine consists of 4 main components: tower, nacelle, hub, blades.

She said I never knew they would be so big, so white so big so white.

In this design the turbine from footing to blade tip stands

over 110 metres. No idea so big, so

taller than a 33 storey building.

A storey = 3.3 metres

dominating towering homes such huge moving white machines turning. Tapered tubular steel tower in three sections

with over 64 tonnes of steel.

So big so white move move all time turn white big blades shimmy horizon make.

Each tower base anchored into position by 300 cubic meters of concrete,

weighing 721.959 tonnes

glimmer gleam in big white slow move all movement.

The nacelle the size of a bus contains yaw system gearbox generator crane.

horizon the still line no longer still horizon calm no longer stillpoint. Rotor blades attached to nodular cast iron hub contains hydraulic pitch system. Nacelle and hub have a combined weight of approximately 65 tonnes disappear peace of day window corner eye blades flick turn 40 metre fibreglass construction blades span more than Boeing 747 jumbo jet wingspan, weigh up to 6 tonnes each. Area swept by blades = pi × radius squared = 5289 square metres. Area of the MCG Oval 17,720 square metres so big so very big how turning how do they start turning blades so heavy big and leaves barely flutter.

The power output of a wind turbine is directly related to the area swept by the blades called the 'capture area' turning the horizon calm stillpoint spins sun power input for cooling heating computers blade activation operational systems not disclosed in specifications the larger the diameter of the blades, the more power it is capable of extracting from the wind hills glint white whiter bright the blades turning turning the still line to movement that still peace serenity disappeared the nominal speed at blade tip = 71.2 metres per second. The speed of sound depending on air temperature is 332 metres per second. shadow stutter Kitchen wall all flicker and sunset flame on wall all flickering flame.

Each turbine requires over 90 tonnes of steel.

1 tonne equals 1000 kilograms when sunsets and I stutter stutter when the lines all move and I stutter and stutter. As the horizon spins.

I.

This model is a smaller design by modern standards: the latest industrial turbines stand over 182 metres tall, 55 storeys, 70 metre blades requiring about eight times as much steel, copper, and aluminium. Spin fall down with the head whirled my world. Energy intensive industries include steel fibreglass cement glass whirled no piece day silent peace all spluttered she.

Blades, nacelle, hub and towers are produced elsewhere and must be transported great distances. Often from overseas.

So big I

didn't think they would be

no longer still kitchen the birdsong calm.

Dan's notes: mid spring

sunset north west wind
shadows flickering kitchen
sun strobing through blades

spring south westerly
2 am. wind ain't rustling
waking chest tight fear

midnight stinking hot
we could not sleep in that room
no open windows

hail shreds leaves, buds
mind drift what did I just read
ants crawl on white page

becalmed, showers
another property bought
throbbing pulse skull chest

icy southerly
it is only in their heads
swoosh swoosh swoosh thump swoosh

An empty barrel sings in the wind.

(Croatian proverb)

SPIN

Angie and Conrad speak out

Each bay its own wind. (Fijian proverb)

a night has harm, swooping on dark reaches, the waves, the waves, slash still air
a pulse, a throb, a hum, a rumble, a roar, a swooshing beat, that defeats sleep
awake with the waves, the waves, that hammer, drive, pierce, the soft snug of rest,
our hearts thunder, alert alarm, our eyes flick dark, ears pin,
wait for intruders heavy breath, snapping step, but a pulse, a hum, a throb
of waves, of waves our cells quiver. our legs twitch. we wait. sleep
distant, pressed from our being, while we wait. our ears hum. our ears ache.
pressure builds. as we wait, we breathe, to calm, we breathe deep and deep,
begging sleep to bless the wearied night, a night that needs no eyes for pass.
we washed out wrung out wave dragged weary. body stiffening into day.
first light beacons birds bellow. sunrise curses. a day begins with little joy.

Dan's notes: late spring

so clear the stars hold
all night turning this way that
body buzz ears hum

                                   intermittent rain
                                   it is not just what you hear
                                   complain to council

foggy morning still
neighbours windows double glazed
quiet sleep real late

                                   south west wind blows hard
                                   another letter of complaint sent
                                   as if hands crush skull

calm, notes in work boots
is windfarm noise compliant
a high pitched whine

                                   blue skies southerly
                                   today mum and dad headaches
                                   company 'no problem'

Gaby

ache beads cellular   small explosions shiver and shake

   we know our flesh in such small ways   familiar agitations

  in the night   we wake   the body   aquiver

paused   poised   a roo waiting stir

   heart   takes   flight   chest fills   straining fright

    mind all tick   a tick   turning over   turning more   and   more

  digging in   rut of everyday   of who   said what to who

    will the   cumin seeds fit   in that   jar   is that   what she said   or did she

will i say yes no   maybe   mean something   else, or what is it

   i need to   do at this point   time   need   cucumbers yoghurt vegemite

sleep   need   sleep   breath   breath   breath

  bake bread   when   slow a twitch leg spasm small

      shift   slow breath

31

Vera

san marzano, rouge de marmande, mortgage breaker,
oxheart, tommy toe, legend, capsicum, peperoncini,
pepadew, capsicum marconi, rosa bianca, greek eggplant,
zucchini tromboncino, zucchini cocozelle, cos, raddichio,

with the years passing, each a year of growing, eating
and returning to the soil, the soil deepens, rich and
thoughtful worms, tunnelling air, turning. each year
the harvest, fresh in summer the sweet smells hover
with bees, linger in the kitchen, add to the calm nights
warm joy. the garden is giving, and Vera is giving.
she tends the garden, digs the soil, composts, mulches.
harvests. cooks. preserves. a life begun, origin
spun in a village, stone homes crag top, her family root
clung centuries, a world away, in time and thought,
speranza sempre. her living is with the earth, all
her living with the earth. hands know the heat,
texture, till, the soil is tended. deep. full with

arugula, basil, broccolini, green calabrese,
romanesco, parsley, cucumbers, spring onions,
sweet corn, peas, butter beans, cavolo nero, spinach,
silverbeet, artichoke, parsnips, beetroot, carrots, swede,

hands skin hard crust crack, know tender, in the
roll of dough, the play of palms, clapped, clipped, held,
when small uncurls *speranza sempre*, spill the water
warm, on soaped soft, a tinyness exhales, the voice
grows tall, and the days tough end in a murmur.
they are planted the children, seed grown strong
and they on the wind away journey, blown some.
she is still stay, in the day to day of it all, in the
house on a hill, a home away, here, in the garden

talk shared neighbourly, from year to year, baskets
bounty balanced borne, amica, afternoons spread
binds, lives on land, a sun up a sun down, stories,
similar and sounding, they are together in the
paddock sprawl, country mile, solitary, there, when
needed, the familiarity of female, not, as in soul
secrets, but as necessity that turns differences to
comfort, and the small of everyday, sticky as jam, with
the years they are to each other kind, and now the
kindness of others, has been spliced by greed, they

turnips, nadine, nicola, desiree, dutch creams,
habanero, corno di toro rosso, yellow cayenne, green
chilli, red marconi, elephant garlic, spanish roja, silver white,
persian star, siciliano, italian purple, georgian crystal,

heed each other's, worn and bleary, thump awake, fright
scuttles sleep, the dreams torn, tatter night of shattered
sleep, they fearfold, huddle inshared, stories of
what the night holds, on wind-drone ice-clear nights, the
bite, and in speaking together, know the other speaking
true, as they too, speak true, of what they, in the homeheart,
place of rest, of soul to soul open/bare, where dreams migrate,
in this place where truth is all, this disrupted, invaded, *speranza*
sempre, they know that to speak abroad of what they know
will not be believed, they know the isolation of their speaking,
they know their bodies pulse, quiver and twitch, the pressure
and pain, in ears, head, chest, all tightening, they know this as
what has happened and still happens, from day to day, night to
night, not every day not every night, but never before the turbines
operated, never before. all spoken over afternoon tea. *speranza sempre*

onions, asparagus, broad beans, romano, borlotti,
purple king, roc d'or, red shallots, comfrey, borage,
hyssop, rosmarino, thyme, chervil, lemon thyme, sage,
chamomile, mint, spearmint, lemon balm, tarragon,

this wear-down, pound, scattering sleep, the day, thought, and no
where when, standing before the cupboard seeking what, swaying
grasp pink formica bench top snow dome fleck tossed, blurring
in this topsy turvey world, belief in a government that protects its
people, shattered, knowledge of big business uncaring ways compound,
profit before people, not the world she knows, not the world of
baskets filled and shared, of doing to their neighbour as they
would have done to themselves, of honesty compassion in all, this
incomprehensible in the round upon round of plea and complaint
to councillors, politicians, The Company, year in year out worn,
warning as she empties shelves drawers cupboards of her breath
her smell her hope that she will not surrender will return home
not let others live like this emptying into suitcases boxes bags
their lives of small things moments memories not much in
the end when the door closed locked, the gate shut locked
the house growing cold in the brisk southerly. *speranza sempre*

Jack

a man has a living to make, way beyond life's
give and take. when the drought struck
we knew we were out of luck.
season after season dragged on
the rain, the clouds, the water all gone.
the dams dry
by and by
a good looking lass from town
flashed her cash around
she had a deal
it was a steal.
our hills may be dry, our dams crack
but wind, wind, wind there was no lack.

a bright new world promised to us
especially if we made no fuss
just listen, heed and believe
cash, security, acclaim receive
our paddocks bare, trodden down
our bank manager only lends a frown
now this company will lease our land
for us to join the green saviours band
turbines will send our kids to the best school
buy another house elsewhere, with a pool
now we've bought our neighbours ground
they left cos of the vibration and the sound
the noise is bad but that company lass
paid for our windows of double glass

windows closed all summer through
now we need an air-conditioner or two
the energy bill gone through the roof
just so we will not hear doof doof doof
so the company lass foots the bill
while the turbines turn on our hill
of course we say they make no noise
when asked by those wind cowboys
we make statements to the media
of how our neighbours, perhaps feel seedier
green, as in jealous, of our new found wealth
not the turbines noise affecting health
we bought that house in another place
to sleep, not disturbed, by that infernal bass.

in all the meetings and promotional blurbs they say
turbines make no more noise than a fridge, a brook, may
be disguised by the sound of rustling leaves.
those who complain of noise are thieves
they would steal our future, our livelihood
make trouble in our neighbourhood
but we who have a vested interest ensure the locals tell
the tale, where turbine noise does not make for living hell
if our parrots do not repeat
the story from the same song sheet
there are ways and means, tried and tested
vile words, cruel rumours, flocks molested,
reminding them of their place and unity
within this close knit happy community.

Daphne and Ted

sixty years married to land home each other
speaks familiarity
know climate of heart paddock hills clouds
south westerly no longer bears
rain not as it once
sentence fall finished each
they beckon dust and dream
afternoons smell carrots scones
days nights tormented/harrowed invaded/plagued
beyond age where calm should settle

complaint no 315 draws mister grey suit
thirtysomething urban company tool slickster
this not his territory
his sedan shoes dusted
his nose chooks sheep shit
at table hospitality spread
explains their complaints
noted numbered
company concerned
their health of concern
have they seen a doctor
perhaps
for the noise that annoys
is not the noise
he hears when he stands briefly
in his opinion they need
to see a doctor
for the noise that they hear
is not a noise state
their experts in
their expert opinion

Troy

bag of wind

I'm here to listen, to listen to you, to listen to your concerns. Yes, really listen. Listen really. A real listening. We know you are anxious. We know you are worried. We know you are hearing. But what are you hearing? You are not listening to what we are telling you that you are hearing. You are telling us that what you are hearing is not what we are telling you that you will hear if you listen in the way we tell you to listen. Really listening. Yes you really need to listen like we listen. And then you will hear, what we hear as we listen.

Now that is the sound of a refrigerator, yes the sound of a modern refrigerator purring way away in your kitchen. Not something you really listen to. Not something you hear. Unless you are worried. Unless you are anxious about this model of refrigerator. New and gleaming and oh so, so technologically advanced. It is quiet, so, so quiet. Nothing to disturb you. Nothing to be worried about. Are you really listening to what I am saying? It sounds like that lovely refrigerator purring way away in your kitchen. A soft, soft sound, so comforting, knowing that it is keeping your greens fresh.

You are saying that is not what you are hearing. Ah, perhaps you are more familiar with the sounds of wind in the trees, the soft so soft susurrations of leaves shivering in the breeze. So comforting, that natural sound of green leaves … or perhaps the sound of a babbling brook. The soothing sound of running water or waves lapping a shore. So calming. So reassuring. So, so quiet. It would send you to sleep. This is what you are listening to. This is what you are hearing. I am telling you that is what you are hearing. Are you listening to me?

Dan's notes: later spring

hard frost northeast breeze
complaint number five hundred
no action as usual

fresh south westerly
neighbours ask how to complain
neck muscles spasm

frost crunch breath cloud ring
no one would want to make this up
am all over the shop

windblown 3 am
the pain in her cry awakes
we are abandoned

moon full creams dark bright
noise optimise the turbines
sleep a human right

light cloud brisk north breeze
political agendas
packing up leaving

Vera at a community lunch

You got a headache   whinger

    a pointer to the head, held like a pistol

You got a headache   hypochondriac

    a thin whine twisting in

You got a headache   jealous

    five sneering faces cluster close
    mouths spit

You got a headache   sick in the head

    spat, splatters
    no return,

You got a headache   envious

    she splits, leaves the spat, collects
    her breath, her bag, her calm,
    they

You got a headache   idiot

    turn back, turn their backs
    on she who knew them so
    long, no longer,
    they

You got a headache   whinger

    she is other
    she is woken up.
    she has a headache.

big red truck

cattle truck   rattling
road hogging too fast centre curving
air brakes squeal cattle tail flicks.
blue ute off narrow cracked pot-
holed edge crumbling crevassed
truck-worn road broken the blue ute
swerving gravel skews dust   craters missed   lives
moments to see the passage   the drivers
eyes glint a mad hint an angry taunt a
short armed flaunt and the heart now
bumps fast   at least   they have passed by
not on   neighbours go by

mist clung paddocks early morning fresh
eyes still warm with dreams the close huddle
of sleep wind clicks cypress row
the cattle low   hallo hallo   cluster
the red truck shakes by all metal clanging
veers off road splatters bins
newspapers spin plastic bags split
spill the remains emptied bags bottles
containers wrappers all fly   no lettuce leaves
banana skin fling the compost's in
the garden rotting quietly
in the warm space where worms live
four dogs erupt alarm although no harm done
to life or limb the garbos following chortle
with the sudden hurtle of
lives exposed

Fay

Since the turbines began spinning, there's
been a hum, in my ears, nOt always,
sometimes worse than others, can be like
a roar, a rumble, inside my head, not like a
loud noise from outside, but inside, inside
of me, in temples, skull, ears, in my bed,
my home. My head pillow plaCed, ear
resting pillow I hear the hum, so clearly feel
in my body, vibration, as if my very cells
were shaking quaking pulsating. My heart
gallops, a herd drums up. I am awake. SO
awake. Startled, look for the stranger over
my bed. Home invader. I feel fear. Want
to run. Home. Safe. No home to go to. It's
been taken. No haven. Not even my body
is safe. There is the black of night. A silence
that is not silence. Sleep does not return.
Serenity, peace, do not return. No home to
return to.

Fern

They wear tin-foil hats to protect them from the noise they cannot hear. You know. Imagine a noise you cannot hear, doing harm. How can something that will save the planet make you siCk? What makes you sick is black and brown and comes from the ground. They get sick, those people who live near mines. Big corporations with vested interests covered up the harm to people same same tobacco, asbestos. Science knew for ages that it caused problems. Now we know we're concerned. Science making neW discoveries will save the planet. Science and scientific thinking that is curious, rigorous, explorative. Not the crazy mixed up politically motivated technologically terrified victims of rightwing tabloid idiot thinking who say they are getting sick because of a noise they feel.

Mitzi

quick, quick, her skin thrums, hotly hotly, a flush runs
through, she runs out, kitchen to car, her hair swept
wild in wind, her eyes flick fast, clock cast late, not too
engine revving late, hard, foot pedals rammed down,
driveway scattered, ravens, gravel fly, a dark flurry
for this woman's worry, a thought pounding round, round
just one thought after the days din, her head throbs, in
side, outside, just one roar, auto fury, for insistent
sound, her heart rattling, as cattle charge, this prattle
too loud, too much noise, there is too much noise,
she explodes into the meeting, they are noisy, too noisy
a sudden stop of money counting, a hush hush now now
too damn noisy, I can't think, can't sleep, turn them off she
spits into the faces circling familiar tutting calm she is an open
mouthed cry begging mercy running from the room tears
a pause eye to eye brow shrugs a shake and sigh rolls the
room turbulence typical in the day to day to and fro the her
they know spirited and sensitive in that boozey way not that
they would say to anyone outside of the inside power
broking the run of community, their community like with
like nothing said or the backs turned the words burn say
nought no drought of affection, of backscratching, patting,
smug and efficient flick of notes, counted dispensed.

Dan's notes: winter

huge winds uproot trees
politicians in denial
haven't slept for days

squalls but little rain
profit before people
ploughing soil and thoughts

too cold to be out
multiple breaches of permit
anxiety swamps

wild wind Sunday roast
all family has headache
no conversation

soft north breeze drizzle
'average' noise level means nothing
hosts have own troubles

clouds cover the hills
another house left empty
they won't talk about it

up 2

that is up too
up up
up to what
watt
can do up to
watt
to what
2 watt
up 2 watt
up to what
can can
do
can do 2 watts up
what can is that
toucan
too can
2 can did
2 can do do
watt
what watt
two cans make watt
what candid toucan
can do
up to
witch what is that
watt whirred
burred
can do up to what
can can
hiss

watt hiss dat
re cord
strangle
holed
strained gull
sheep wreck
ha ha ha
hell hiss hear
it hertz

Wind and fortune are not lasting.

(Portuguese proverb)

Fay speaks of spin

they spin do spin spun spin spin forward,
do spin around round spin forward round
whirred spinning turning spun spin sizzling
speed fast towards bright, bright of future,
do future past present tense forward future
whirred round round spun right bright
round, all words worlds spinning future
clean, spun round no track trace empty
out ground vapid space, whirled round,
empty out mind, empty out moral, floral,
towards spin spun bind borrowed time,
of the future of time in the future, turning
fast future spins round, spinning it up
spinning around whirled future around
empty words towards all hollow borrowed
floral sounding bright future do spin forward
spin do around spin around words bind
future no trace space round words bright
do bright clean spin future round words
borrowing future turn empty they towards
sizzling they do spin sizzling forwards spin
toward clean bright empty spun words spun
empty out world future

words on wind ears wide open

that old bloke again   chop the greens   down viewing platform
don't want   two   with his sign   know more   don't put
it there wind turbines   she just has   i don't think they know
everyone under her thumb   what they are talking about who   the hell
them smaller   i don't feel like it   he's probably a pensioner   did you hear
me   people just want to believe   i'm   tired   government handouts   if you
don't live here   how would you know   you don't need income   chop those
greens smaller   they want the world saved   well where do i put it   i didn't
sleep last night   you got to earn a living   sleep   more like dice   i told you
where to put   he should shut   it   are you stupid   up   the bloody
instructions are   i'm going   there   down there   can't you read
if not   they'd believe   we'll teach   anything   him   it's a religion
don't yell   she can   at me   be   such a mean bitch   i'm going to get
me   i've got   a posse   a   that's good   headache   darling

Mattie

can't settle today can't settle

wind in my bonnet bees on breeze

nothing continues except a shift shake wondering

what long and shuddering fall of thought body tree

nowhere so much as here now and the other turning

the trough amplified where the snouts low sucking

bellow below the pack the scrum the scum cycle

the peak not mounted passed

things don't stick in my head neither pin nor word basic

structures articulated imprecise failing poetics science

rigour conjugating experience rough shod hell bent

tempo crashed the jangle jarred the upbeat downturned

matter pending order desire for sleep embedded

state twitched prickled squeezed

succour sucker been suckered

Dan's notes: early autumn

total fire ban
systemic regulatory failure
clanking clunking gears

hot blustery wind
no interest in living
last night fence wire cut

scurrying rain wind
who shut gate, sheep no water
pain in the temples

rosellas squawking
a no win situation
thin skinned fractious, spent

fingers of pale light
turbine blades locked together
cannot concentrate

storm looms horizon
no respite in our kitchen
you go out of your mind

Cassandra

not prophecy but what lies beyond the gates as my eyes see it as I feel, a feeling like none before or in no other place, a feeling that now belongs to what I know of home. home being a place for feeling. feeling safe allowing all feelings form and expression but this feeling not metaphysical nor emotional though emotion now becoming attached and having its own sense of feeling this feeling with many shifting subtleties being feelings acting within my flesh and skeleton. bones know these feelings as do the cells and atoms of my existing. some crisis here in intimate space from beyond the gates.

I am hearing of others also who are experiencing feelings different from anything they had felt before and we have spoken together of that which we are experiencing and are surprised to find the feelings, the feelings in our flesh bones cavities, echoing, echoing what we each are feeling, feeling in our bodies in our homes, the place that now these feelings are there, is no longer feeling as safe as houses. we are no longer feeling safe and having spoken together, speak to those who we believe concerned to hear will act.

though we are speaking we are still questioning questioning the feelings those feelings in flesh bone cavity we are experiencing and wondering how we could be feeling this that we are feeling so questioning what else what else it could be what else that we here just now in this place in this area began experiencing at a similar time and without talking each to the other and then discovering discovering through one saying to another and then that one to another and then knowing many who on the one day headaches earaches nausea and for each one and one and one it is new and unfamiliar wondering how this could be and only one thing having changed for all of us at the time the change in our environment and we are asking how it could be for authorities standards guidelines protect people yes they are there for protecting people we say but having each felt what each is feeling and sharing this and hearing of others also experiencing the feelings same but not same feeling know that authorities standards are not are not there to safeguard.

we are speaking together of the worry we have for the feelings in our flesh and bones, of the worry we feel for others who may be experiencing these feelings more than feelings where for nights when the wind when the wind blowing on the hills here at our homes downstream no wind all still we pummelled sleep fractured heart pound our heads ears bodies pressure filled pain and days of minds emptying in unknotting phrases words falling failing feelings.

we are speaking to people of what we are experiencing feeling in our bodies flesh bone cavity so that others will not have to experience these feelings that we are experiencing we are telling those who have a responsibility to safeguard the people what we are experiencing we are telling them carefully and precisely of this that has been happening only since the turbines began turning and turning but those who would safeguard people are not listening are not believing that which we say we are feeling each in our bodies are not asking questions are not investigating we are warning of a problem that we each are feeling in our bodies so that this problem will not be repeated they are not believing because they do not want to believe that which would upset what it is they believe and want to believe. this is a story that has been told before a mistake that has been made too often we seeing agendas all sides agendas and all sides reluctance for the questioning that challenging the way we are seeing the world, questioning challenging the lens of our way of seeing the world our world beliefs and that it is questioning that grows us our understanding questioning opening dialogue discussion and we so small without this.

when our bones cells flesh knowing denied dismissed we are all reduced as humans when our homes are trespassed by others we all reduced as humans my small voice no longer knows home, the haven of body and place we betrayed abandoned this is not the first time nor the last where humans choose to believe that which does not challenge their world as they are seeing it.

this is the story we hear, we are hearing from here, there, across the waters in many lands in many languages people telling the story of what they are experiencing, feeling in their flesh bones cavities, telling of this experience and this telling not wanting to be heard nor believed not heard not heeded not believed dismissed denied. they are telling the people who should be listening. the people who are there to protect. they are telling politicians corporations doctors journalists. they are repeating the telling and many who should act as well as listen do not. they do not. and those that do, they too are not heeded.

Leon

heart constricts. you know that physically tightening, clenching

fist. the heart a clenched fist. so many closed faces when my heart tightens.

Oh. titans of industry vested interest, purse strings, clamp politicians, yank those

puppets strings, draw strings draw tight. set circumference, inner circle, spin. circle snap

shut close. Oh. what is said in the inner circle remains in the inner circle that which is released,

cleansed, spins. a cycle of spin never turned returned spinning out public air public realm what

is said is out, what is out is said and what is out is believed never turned returned even if nipped

pruned refuted. Oh. the spin cycles tightening heart clenched fists the heart pounds. what is not said is

not. what is not written is not. what is hidden is not. what is obscured is not. what is not is not. all

knots. Oh. a circle of knots tightening. once out good as true. never turned spin cycles circles public.

when all is said the done is. done done do done. done to. been done over. Oh. inner circle spin cycles

puppet strings snap tight shut close inner titans sphincter clutched constructs the spin said debate.

not debate. knot tight not turn return. constrict construct. good as true. spin cycle frenzy

inform inform misinform disinform noise cycling titans interest what is said is out out is

gospel. Oh. spin cycles the fabric unravels knot the circle closed heart tightening

clenching fists unknotting strings. Oh. all this noise. the spin cycle noisy.

take a proper gander will you. white noise parakeets paraphrase

propaganda titan spin cycle fact check. rich

the froth rich the dye

rich. Not fat

cheque.

Cast.

Oh.

Charles and Una

i) family round table weigh each consider to and fro as active as any
   drought no rain no water cash flow drying stock dying all change
   world climate people money change we are farmers exchange view
   company spruiks great rewards little sound no disturbance review
   shrivelling shoots parched paddocks in balance future be solution
   renew hope world survival our children's children depend

ii) shearing shed sounds out
    delivering hay shaking his head
    aches in air press push pulse
    how do you live with this?

iii) regrets are more than shadows flickering kitchen sinks sun pressure
    building inner ear temple thorax neighbour sleep trampled wave
    upon wave pounding this is not what we were told repeating in the
    nights empty chasm nothing to be done now

iv) moon scrap scrapes black eery
    awake when all earth sleeps sheep
    account no balance
    how can I live with myself?

Dan's notes: mid winter

south easterly wind
leaves hang, blades bent back, spill wind
dad's guts are boiling

still at ground level
blades rotating fast, thumping
it might be wind shear

rain maybe later
wilfully blind health bodies
can't think straight feel vague

early nancy's out
experience not theory
they don't understand

tranquil blue one cloud
again authorities fail
in duty of care

still, small peace this noon
just collateral damage
nothing you can do

Cassandra speaks of Fay

she was so brave to speak in such a situation what was i doing stop
think washing on the line rain now we always want rain whether the
washing he dismissed her on the line although mouthing the platitude
of understanding he not understanding dismissed her before all those
people such a blustery day slanting he assumed rain sleet stooping he
knew too late for the washing assumptions mask any possibility of
understanding and that in thinking one knows insults cruel cruel so
cruel for those suffering for those so disregarded even the wind so cold
for spring ice in its breath and all she wanted to say there is a problem
beware beware to warn washing will tear in how many years will they
know science will say yes there is a problem oh we didn't know we
thought those people at that time were the rain lessening the wind
whipped we thought they were on the other side driven by dark motives
see how the garden already greens and shines that they on the other
side the clouds moving fast see sides seeing sides divides and in that
division lays the ground of distrust we so distrust how honeyeater turf
war what a cacophony can a person assume they know what motivates
you listen to that noise they dive each other look at refugees muslims
women blacks lgbts they know too well the way some people assume all
muslims terrorists all blacks violent all women less all dot dot dot are
spotted watch as they dart and dash through how those who assume
they know the washing rain rinsed look so smugly superior wait for the
sun though the wind how can a person stand before you after hearing
what you have said tattered fraying and tell you that you are wrong even
though they have no experience never lived a half life where the jots
never join how can people be so cruel she was so brave the sun is out
now to speak in that situation

clasp knot

do not clASp
poISon words
deLIVEred when
your body shaKEN
not preSENT
they
divide

the unkNOWn
do not kNOw
know only
authORised
knowLEDge
$$$
count

wHEN
people
procLAim
propaGANda
true
as blue
skies humanity/we/hEARts/minds
die

when

there

is

NO

place

to

question

thERE is

no freeDOm

of

speech

poISon

propagANDa

prevAILS

Eat the wind and swallow bitterness.

(Portuguese proverb)

TORQUE

a roo ral lamming Tay shun

O ye that put yore tRust and con Fee dance in guv meants core poor a shun BU row cats hex spurts 4 (h)ire as goons 4 ire as myrrh sin rees

re member deaf hand loke uh on mi

this raid e us ov in flu ents know pro tech shun four or din airy pee pull

do they plays pee pull prince E pals bee 4 own inter rests bee four prophet, take care ov da small purse sun?

no imbaLance of power inn eq qui tea be twin

hoo r da ga dee aeons hoo r da hex spurts

Dusty and Lou

We lost our home, our dream home.
    My husband and I bought the farm.
    We wanted to plant trees.
    We wanted to watch the stars.
    We wanted to sit on the veranda on summer
    evenings, watch the mountains shadow, listen
    to the land drawing breath after the heat of the day.
    We took ages to buy that farm.
    That was the place we wanted to be.

Then turbines, 56 within 1.5 kilometres erected, each 120 metres tall.

The developer said there would be no problems.
Department of Planning said, 'We didn't know you were there.'
We had no idea.

Then flashing lights, strobing in the morning,
strobing in the evening. Panic
attacks. The moon rose through
the blades. The sun.
We could not look at the stars.
We could not sit on the veranda.
Some nights were as if a jet plane never passed.
We could not sleep.
We wore headphones, with music.
We thought we were going crazy.
I went to the doctor:
    'I don't know what's wrong
    with me. I'm not sick, but
    I don't feel well.' I do not
    go to the doctor very often. He said:
    'Well, what's changed in your environment?
    What's changed with your life?'

The only thing that had changed was the turbines.

So many times people say your problem is:

You are a NIMBY

You are selfish

You haven't got a financial interest

You are jealous

You are stupid

You are a part of the tin foil hat brigade

You are afraid

You are crazy

You are a wing nut

You don't like the way they look

You are anxious

You are a climate change denier

You are a flat-earther

You are a servant of Big Coal

You are a dick brain

You are a moronic victim of Right Wing Tabloids

You are a hypochondriac

You are a luddite

You are loony tunes

You are an envious whinger

You are responsible for the end of the world.

We know what we feel. We know what is affecting us.
We planted trees to grow nuts not go nuts.

I met Leon, Mattie and their family. They were having exactly the same problems.
Acoustic testing in our lounge was off the scale.
It was crazy. It was off the planet. Like theirs.
Off the planet.

This was after I had first been to the doctor.

I was curled up on the couch a doona over my head, thinking,
    'I just want to die.'
    I do not suffer from depression.
    My doctor said, 'Are you going
    to self-harm?' 'Don't be stupid
    I said, I'm too much of a coward,'
    he said to me, 'Get the hell out of there.'

I wrote hundreds of letters to politicians, bureaucrats and
what do I get back? 'There's no evidence that
these things affect you. If you have health
issues, you should see your doctor.'

Since we left our home, we can
sleep now, not bone weary day in
day out, struggling for words, vitality
feeling like life worthless my heart
though broken in every way, shape form
In every way, my life turned upside down.

I am thankful that The Company bought
us out. And yes, I am under
a gag agreement.

There is no doubt the turbines, nothing else,
affected us. People choose not to listen do not
prick up their ears sound out their ears muffled
by the comfort of their beliefs most do not live
with turbines they choose to dismiss deny denigrate

    I do not know why.

    I have to speak out.

    This cannot go on.

noise

all animals need to be alert to threats even when they are asleep,
so they can wake up and flee, if necessary

nOisecancreatea

formofChroNic

stressthatkeepsOurbodiesin

astate   ofconstantAlert

nOisecanaggravate

StressStillfurther   ifitdisturbssleep

resultingin   constantfat   iguecognitiveimp   airment

irritabilitydepression

No ise   dis turbed   s leep

Mustbe con sidered asapart icular   pot   ential

Path   wayfor   the deV   elopment of

Card   io   vas   cu lar   dis   orders

Imp   aired   imm   unity

Asud den loud noise will wake you.

The ear re sponds tothe peaks of Sound, not ave rages.

Thou Sands ofpeople   worldwide re

porting ad   verse health abasisOf   empirical knowledge.

The nervous system the most sensitive instrument.

So much we do not know.

even when you are asleep, your ears, brain and body
continue to react to sounds, raising levels of stress
hormones such as cortisol, adrenalin and
noradrenalin.

Dan's notes: summer

no water for stock
neighbours forced out of their home
too tired to speak

more hot air rips land
industry propaganda
pressure builds in ears

red sun horizon slung
nothing to do with compliance
noise knows no borders

midday burns no wind
big money on the table
to speak out no more

heat wrinkles the day
threatened, haystacks burnt overnight
where is my notebook

turbines not turning
regulatory capture
money to be made

what hurts

watt hertz will the pain doubled da bulled a rest arrest the air hair split hum that drives
that drives from in a inner outer crays craze of shell sock ears muffler   oar the tinny wine
etching fine what hurts watt hertz s c r amble ·   the b rain can t be gin re
member   all on win   d   torn tat turd sin seer sore   head   no-ing   the
turd   will hit the   big fan   sum   sea   greed   sum   c   scents
udders   sea   fun da   meant Alists udders poe   li   tickle a genders
what hurts   watt hertz thunder   a   storm   parsing   Alists funder winned
one dah on the   4   sure   war tars   rising   ware   you   tense   hills
        washed   inn   old b 4 now   muscles   pail   whether vial   raise seize
wear reign kneaded it knot   awful offal few jure by thyme his   story   icing   paw   paw
pop you lace 4   peas for peace   throw a   pore shun 2   mi   watt hertz
pee pull inequity watt hertz pee pull know stake the   porpoise piece   knot   proper
gander buy the whey   the whale   and whine from eye sum won and udders   tolled
true moor   hi   prays   knot tolled sow
buy holey mother whirled maid bye bye grid new rite A weigh cents tolled bi udders
spanner inner works throne threw spinner no moor truth tolled all sensor lye too toad line
proper gander

                    fundament
                    fundamentalist
                    fundamental ist
                    funder mental list
                    funder meant a list
                    funder meant a less
                    funder men taa list
                    fun da mental list
                    fun da men to list
                    fun da meant less
                    thunder mental list
                    thunder meant less
                    thunder men to list
                    thunder mental
                    thunder meant
                    thunder men a hiss

Dan's notes: mid summer

insanely blue sky
everyone knows no one says
the guts to stand up

                                   grey clouds bank hill top
                                   across the world same story
                                   wilful disregard / denial

continual drip
croney capitalism
disturbing the peace

                                   north west heavy rain
                                   no accountability
                                   lack of inquiry

thick mist silence close
self regulation a farce
can't keep going on

                                   sun shower silvers
                                   dogmatic creed makes them blind
                                   always anxious now

Evan

Here is my bedrock, the locus of my life. A small home of stone in a small village of stone, amongst hills of stone, where people have laid slate, limestone, sandstone, bluestone to keep safe family, faith, and future for a thousand years. On Sunday the church bells still summon belief although the genuflection may be in gardens to roses, or on a hillside to a spring yet the bells place us. As do the calls and laughter of children. We are a village that still has children, a school, and their sound spills over, promises a future, here where the rivers collide. That lap splash tumbling rumble shaped passage for centuries and we here now, as they here then, listening and sipping in the water-freshened air. Singing sometime. All together singing with the low approach of tones merging, as river, children, bells, stone folding in a home range. We live in this confluence. So when they said twenty turbines were to be built in the stone hills behind my stone house, I welcomed them as being part of our continuing. The developers assured us the windmills would cause hardly any disturbance, for each of us in our homes and school and workplaces here in our small village. The sounds of our home range not disturbed. But once the blades began to turn, once they began to shift with the wind, a fault-line erupted, it was as if someone were mixing cement in the sky. I could not be in my garden any more. Two neighbours, whose sleep had been solid now knew disturbance, a nightly toss and turn. Their eyes darkened, as did their spirits and they became ill. We complained, appealed, spoke out. Who listens? After four years of complaints and appeals to the company and governments who have ears of stone, we left our home, our bedrock of seventeen years.

Dan's notes: very late summer

hot, rain later, plough
phoned in complaint
constant hum in ears

upper wind still here
company staff say, shouldn't
you see a doctor

steamy dusk no breeze
another cycle of spin
more talk no action

windy on hills, extreme
amplitude modulation
can't get back to sleep

still night turbines thump
predicted noise inexact
just can't find the word

rain till the ground seeps
media ignores scandal
heightened noise zones

T1, T2, T3 converse

Three turbines, brothers of the knighthood, knaves in the Order of Shift and Spin:

Gam! few gimcracks proper yaff knights nay so green. Solo grind when wind blows, require baseload, backup alltime, be dingable, lumb noisy, eyesore, baste bats, birds. Oh that hurts, yours truly can nay carry coals. Knights shoot the breeze, stillstand iota. There be browse mornings, hard doings. Be nay lubberland. We be spin slaves, celebrious saviours of the world as we wit it. Them-uns philistines.

Bro, hast the buzz puckered thou? It haint all gospel chat. A downy cove vardy we-uns ram jam cheek by jowl, naught elbow room, slopes lumb steep, wrong 'un place along of chop and change plan, wuzzled build. Ipso facto turbulency, dead air, gear catever. Bumblecrew close file. Keep it clear as mud. You don't put Lawrie to shepherd the cacklers ken. Be there jobbery, double shuffle, cross?

Git! heartbleeds blab dispersions. "From hatch to dispatch knights steel, aluminium, cement, plastics, fibreglass, rare earth minerals, all mined, carried, processed, manufactured, cracks environs, poisons water, air, makes deadly toxical scaff 'n raff, scrunch folk, CO_2 a suspicion sconced, outweighing windfall of we-uns spin slave cycle." Be we energy laundering racket? 'Taint yours truly funeral.

Nuf ced gyrotwistive gabblegrinders, thou noise be noise be noise annoys. Com-rogues there be no stash to this cruel confounded conflabberation. Yours truly be in a right brown study. Stag and party-line small oats in this carry witchet mumpsimus. It be pollycon hot 'tatie. Deadly haggle how save climate, boom, biz, consume, future. Bottom facts world our crib. Earth Blue Blanket wilds creatures folk altogether yoked, breathe same air.

From years past, hisnabs Gaia cove the earth all omnium gatherum be, creatures great small, hills and rivers, we-uns all clan, inkled dead cert heat is on. We be untwisted, now gone by, tipped over. Must act P.D.Q. Choke off noxious gases, lumb populosity. Big country wilds required for fit as fiddle planet. Require better than technobubble n hairpin flint in. Transmogrify kidney, lingo, institutions. Long term lay, skeet deeds.

Thou woolley crowned windsucker time for crackjaw philosophising be alive gone. Thou bouzhi heartbleed get a grip. Dead to rights big-endian bling bling rescue holus bolus planet be the crack. Simple calculations, green boom traffick be cockall. Earth be dicker goods. Markets boom. Be gear galore. Plunder preserves earth. Plank green boom build green perks for worldwide folk. Biz per usual.

Bro be that a sell! Traffickers egg folk consume for boom. There be an end to earth's goods. Boom consume perish the pact. Can't purchase world to save it. What feather of folk be we? Logrolling bumblecrew be cold as charity. Big Pharma, Vee Dub, bubble co fake data, research doctored. Trumpet bene for folk, bene for planet. It be bogus play, pinchbeck. Who else? Will green boom scheme alone quash environmental wanion?

Bro way back environmental ABC's be, folk pipe peregal, wrinkle elfen in world. Now hijacked. Be green boom, big funds chinse. Long time now, Almighty Gold clean collared grist of geese 'n golden eggs, gear, environs. No care beyond booty. An fossil fuel bloomin' fox paw then choke off. An graball flock guttle, make a peasekill then choke off. An we-uns scumber in very own nest, choke off. Chop chop.

Planet earth jing-bang jiggered up, less folks put their shoulder to the wheel, tighten belts. Them-uns devoirs just consume a dash, bynge luke. Aim, plot, build, castle, industry, victuals, energy, carriage systems, earth friendly. Just rampallion rag gorgers rake in heaps booty. Let alone fat cats feather nest. Ergo status quo. Oodles flat broke better n better desperately bush'd. Ghastly schism large, getting larger. Where be just ass?

Thou agonizing augurs, windy air mongers mang bumper green boom bunnick world and wifes scrape. Require boom for gear, require green for planet. Folk consume better all green be tip top gif gaf, nay throw back to Dark Ages. Thou be good gyro gabblers hold your gulsh. Take a back seat. The knights be on the grumbles. We-uns sit be at stake, else put about gup thou shaky atrocity. Thou scrapped, stew in own juice.

Bros be flash to every move on the board. In all walks world over scuddick pellucidity. The biz, wire-pulling jimjams, dumng dot, flat-move. Bumble crew play fast and loose. Common plug in a fog. Planet n folk needs at odds with Almighty Gold monstrous moreish for mammon. Top dog sway, filthy lucre n me me me prime. Bottom fact, all creatures great n small require plump currant planet. Boom consume fritter boom, be it green or nay, what's the damage?

Few folk care not a bean to sconce so tothers have better, so planet be on the up and up. Top of desire be me n more. Bar green boom backs altogether folk worldwide bonanza. Act green consume green be the far and away green way forward. An folk get up behind green gospel there be toll-ollish planet accommodate 9 billion folk plus. Goods and environs safeguarded. Bros caper skower. Future plummy. Wind dropping.

All is not gold that glitters. Boom consume, green or nay haint the saviour. There be bounds to growth. Clean potato capsize this boom bamboozle devil may care shivaroo. Jaum, negotiate truth and justass deeds, fair rations for folk and planet. Piggot from prime human belongings; ethicks, age old ken, spanfire viewpoints, imagination, a masterpiece future. Big vision, gritty good wooled action. Marestails thinning. Wind dying.

Be Hobson's choice. Can't go on as we be going. Can there be compassion, care n respect for folk n planet toto? Can folk accompany jibe? Not either or, us them, have have not, gangs. Can folk pull together? Can there be a solid move to deeds, true, level headed, inside, respectful? Can we condog on ABC beam parity for folk n planet? Jaum a jannock open house world? Big nuts to crack. Nix wind. We-uns hung up.

Dan's notes: autumn

rare south easterly
elites control information
body vibrating

sound in the landscape
can't reduce to specific
decibel level

west tending north west
complaint number one thousand
feeling nauseous

creeks running high swift
planning permits not enforced
arrhythmic heart beat

clouds stretch sky endless
twitching feet jerks legs awake
feeling so hopeless

paddocks crackle white
windfarms have own signature
who do you believe?

No matter how the wind howls,
the mountain will not bow to it.

(Chinese proverb)

TILT

civilised world

civil eyes whirled hole sale ex ploy station earth devastation water contamination tock sick waist deforestation land grab acid rain oh zone hole in the life cycle ex stink shun in dust tree all civil eyes a shun damage damage damage earth people home why in this civilised world consume con waste more more food energy water than just about every where time one else fritter more food energy water than just about everywhere time weigh ware one why one else hunger injustice destruction while chips cola cakes civil eyes more packaging plastics tee vees smart phones computers games fridges washing machines driers mattresses microwaves coffee makers toasters blenders fluorescent lights batteries can openers thrown out down out wasted why just unjust in this civil eyes whirled want and need (interchangeable) have settled in the same shopping basket by me buy me why up to half all food after production world-wide wasted in this civil eyes world plastic filled albatross pelican gull turtle fish oceans of rubbish past the tipping point clouds heavy with information why whirled powerful festered interests stand in way of planet needs peoples needs a fairer more prosperous world just unjust what a strange echo chamber we live in inequality growing why great idol faith in capitalism as economic social and ethical system culturally unjust inequitable gap between richest and poor increasing just unjust in this civil eyes why a society just/unjust unjustifiable self indulgence self aggrandizement culture flourish live in perpetual dishonesty degrades spirit humanity we are stuck in this civil eyes whirled economic model demands unfettered expansion wake up planet needs people needs question the logic of growth mantra why contract use of resources world wide circular economy material capture reuse frugal clever as ecosystem in this civilise threaten elite minority stranglehold over economy political process and media world why wake them up benefit majority planet in this civilised world wake up civil eyes just

Dan speaks out

there is no end to dis
appointment when trans
parency tinted corporate
narratives souled out earth
people beliefs
we were shopped

there is no end to dis
grace when account
ability gnawed hollow man
ipulated flex
ible figures
we were shopped

no end to dis
honesty in de
sire for never-
ending con
sumption
humanity shopped / we (were) shopped

no end to dis
possession when pro
fit margins rule
land divided dev
eloped those whose ancestors' bones buried there can no
longer live there

no end to dis
advantage
when 80 per
cent of the world's pop
ulation share 5.5 per
cent of the world's wealth

no end to dis

trust

no end to dis

may

no end to dis

prove

no end to dis

illusion

there is an end to dis

courage

when

there is an end to dis

respect

when

there is an end to dis

connect

speaking out

let us imagine we are travelling and passing through a strange and dangerous country

i heard

these voices

softly meek downturned glance strangers she mother wife farmer shy in word and
look stirred by injustice fiercely speak to authority who would tiny her politician CEO
manager no doors closed to she outspoken strong insistent respect our heartland
protect our home

one voice small forms in fight strength   she will be listened to

her steadfast gaze fearless

childhood illness formed him   tribe othered   the grain of his voice ignored   stirred
by injustice gathers knowledge voraciously spreading this truth to everyone he
believes should know and in knowing act unyielding before those who would belittle
him undismayed he stood

one voice small forms in fight strength   he will be listened to

strength in thousand conflicts proves

open armed she offering ear and aid for ill-used careworn heart-broken her cloak
would shield them all stirred by injustice she digs out buried knowledge   questions
unites with others who seeing clearly beyond false notions perpetuated by those who
would little them dare to fight for what is right no matter

one voice small forms in fight strength   she will be listened to

i'm with you

resolve forged he will to safety carry those vulnerable downtrodden   hammer
through all obstacles   if not one way then another   stirred by injustice his speak
straight stand rallies   he knows together determined overcomes

one voice small forms in fight strength   he will be listened to

i'm with you   go boldly

stirred by injustice small voices burgeon power as she guides them to own voice true
and strong she side by side encouraging dare rise up before those that would little
them while she backroom organise detail spread letters news support hour by hour year by year

one voice small forms in fight strength

i'm with you   go boldly

they will be heard

small voices in the world of big denied then the black winged messenger stirred by
injustice delves deep into dark recesses dirty dealings bears their stories for all to hear
and when challenged by those who would scarce him

come friend i have an old story to tell you

one voice small forms in fight strength

one voice strong gains another

i'm with you   go boldly

they will be heard

laughing she will not be deterred by those who would little her knowing she standing
ground linked arm in arm in arm in arm across the seas with those stirred by injustice
to reveal this shame to its bones

one voice small forms in fight strength

one voice strong gains another

i'm with you   go boldly

her steadfast gaze fearless

strength in thousand conflicts proves

we will prevail

mind undisturbed by wind or words patiently observes till the hidden currents surface
and clear-eyed mindful discipline challenges false beliefs within self and others   then
strikes with force and gritty words precisely chosen at the injustice of those who
would little them

one voice strong gains another   we will prevail   go boldly

Sow the wind, reap the whirlwind.

(proverb from Hosea 8:7)

afterword

I first knew berni janssen as a sound artist, about ten years ago while she performed a series of her poems at a music-improvisors community event in Melbourne. I have a vivid memory of that reading – her voice was lyrical, textured and enthusiastic, and the tone both of her spoken-sound and poetry-content was contagious, grin-inducing and also powerful. She has a strong theatrical presence surging through her voice and her words. I do not remember the content of that event from over a decade ago; only the feel or vibe of her reading. Her voice is confident and multi-faceted. I am left smiling, bowled over, sermonised and sung into her world. As a performer her physical, theatrical and creative presence is an intrinsic part of the message. She takes over a space, propelling the words as sound with distinct rhythm and breath. These were my initial impressions, that still remain and are now amplified by the further phases of her work.

More recently, I visited berni again at her home, one hour's drive from where I now live in rural Victoria. She inhabits a self-made, highly creative space surrounded by bushlands. There is roughness and sophistication, and a lifetime as a thinker, collector, and observer. Her space is a physical manifestation of the artistic energy I witnessed years before. Only now (at five years ago) there is a new concern: the giant wind-farms that have been planted in great swaths across our mutual landscape. I had noticed these towering white giants only in the form of two windmills outside my own town that contribute energy to the grid; and I also had some experience from my home landscape in Texas of the controversies that can erupt; some people love the idea of wind power, and some complain about the destruction of their 'view shed' (as Texans are prone to say). What I did not know was that there are multiple arrays of these industrial windmills built into our own landscape, looming dangerously close to people's dwellings and life patterns. berni and her partner pointed out (on that visit five years ago) that the thrumming of the windmills can disturb people's sleep, cause panic attacks, and wreak profound physiological and psychological damage. I did an experimental drive up to the base of one of the white giants, and felt a brief un-nameable disturbance in the body. I could immediately tell that this industrial intrusion would be un-liveable with over any period of time. I was aware that berni and many others in the area were working intensively at exposing and dismantling this encroaching industrialisation of the landscape, which includes the very texture and density of the atmosphere.

Now in the present (2018) I have the honour of previewing berni's book *between wind and water: in a vulnerable place* which I have come to appreciate as her life's work of the past eight years. It is multi-layered and multi-vocal. There are elements of the manifesto, the sermon, the biting exposé, the microscopic appreciation of sensory detail. A vitriolic critique of The Company sits up against detailed observations – and love – of the fragile landscape in which we live, its foods, its plants and local characters. And that ecosystem includes our very own bodies, as the work of capitalism affects everything down to our dreams at night, whether we can find shelter by sleeping on the floor, whether we can afford to move or will resolve to stick it out in place.

The shape of this work is multi-vocal, multi-rhythmed, playful and elegant in its changes of density and texture. When berni read to me, a couple of weeks ago from the just-formatted manuscript, I could see and hear a full theatre of voices arranged in space, dialoguing in twos and threes, monophonic and polyphonic, and (especially) raging in solo voice. There is one patch of text that equals any manifesto I've heard or read yet. Her work is an opera of the imagination.

Loosely discussing the readings, I found myself thinking, on an interior level, "what is all this about, this project of promoting creativity and spirituality? What is it about?" And then (in the wake of berni's reading) that the overarching world-shaping paradigm under which we all now live is essentially a web of variegated forms of capitalism, which goes right into the pores of our thinking and working and living. berni's work manages to both assail the tall, elegant white giants and the nasty corporate wealth-worshipping impulses behind them, while at the same time giving the reader – and listener! – hope and life. Her work bristles with enthusiasm for living and for the small, green things, just as she goes fangs bared and voice rhythmically insistent, out to expose the degradation of our environment.

Catherine Schieve

If you would like to know more about
Spinifex Press, write to us for a free catalogue, visit our
website or email us for further information
on how to subscribe to our monthly newsletter.

Spinifex Press
PO Box 105
Mission Beach QLD 4852
Australia

www.spinifexpress.com.au
women@spinifexpress.com.au